KNOCK-KNOCK JOKES

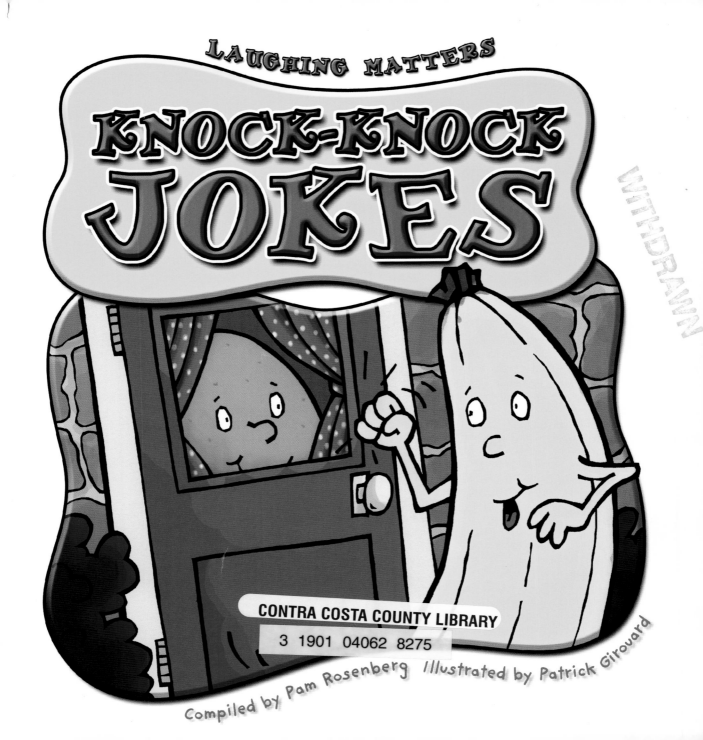

Compiled by Pam Rosenberg   Illustrated by Patrick Girouard

Special thanks to Katie Cottrell for her assistance in compiling source materials.

Published in the United States of America by The Child's World®
P.O. Box 326, Chanhassen, MN 55317-0326
800-599-READ
www.childsworld.com

Acknowledgments

The Child's World®: Mary Berendes, Publishing Director

Editorial Directions, Inc.: E. Russell Primm, Editorial Director and Line Editor; Katie Marsico, Assistant Editor; Matthew Messbarger, Editorial Assistant; Susan Hindman and Susan Ashley, Proofreaders

The Design Lab: Kathleen Petelinsek, Designer and Page Production

Registration

Library of Congress Cataloging-in-Publication Data
Rosenberg, Pam.
  Knock-knock jokes / compiled by Pam Rosenberg ; illustrated by Patrick Girouard.
      p. cm. — (Laughing matters)
  Summary: A collection of simple knock-knock jokes.
    ISBN 1-59296-075-8 (alk. paper)
    1. Knock-knock jokes. 2. Wit and humor, Juvenile. [1. Knock-knock jokes.
  2. Jokes.] I. Girouard, Patrick, ill. II. Title. III. Series.
    PN6231.K55R63   2004
    818'.602—dc22   2003018085

Knock Knock.
Who's there?
Adore.
Adore who?
Adore stands between us. Open up!

Knock Knock.
Who's there?
Adam.
Adam who?
Adam up and tell me the total.

Knock Knock.
Who's there?
Ammonia.
Ammonia who?
Ammonia little kid.

Knock Knock.
Who's there?
Alex.
Alex who?
Alex-plain later.

Knock Knock.
Who's there?
Ahmed.
Ahmed who?
Ahmed a big mistake coming here!

3

Knock Knock.
Who's there?
Ben.
Ben who?
Ben knocking on this door all morning!

Knock Knock.
Who's there?
Boo.
Boo who?
Please don't cry. It's just a joke!

Knock Knock.
Who's there?
Before.
Before who?
Before I freeze to death, please open the door!

Knock Knock.
Who's there?
Banana.
Banana who?
Knock Knock.
Who's there?
Banana.
Banana who?
Knock Knock.
Who's there?
Orange.
Orange who?
Orange you glad I didn't say banana?

Knock Knock.
Who's there?
Bean.
Bean who?
Bean here for ages. What's kept you?

4

Knock Knock.
Who's there?
Duane.
Duane who?
Duane the bathtub,
I'm drowning!

Knock Knock.
Who's there?
Dewey.
Dewey who?
Dewey have to
keep saying all
these jokes?

D

Knock Knock.
Who's there?
Dozen.
Dozen who?
Dozen anyone
want to let me in?

Knock Knock.
Who's there?
Diploma.
Diploma who?
Diploma is here
to fix the sink.

Knock Knock.
Who's there?
Don Juan.
Don Juan who?
Don Juan to go
to school today.

Knock Knock.
Who's there?
Europe.
Europe who?
Europe to no good!

Knock Knock.
Who's there?
Eddie.
Eddie who?
Eddie body home?

E

Knock Knock.
Who's there?
Freddie.
Freddie who?
Freddie or not,
here I come.

F

Knock Knock.
Who's there?
Ferdie.
Ferdie who?
Ferdie last time,
open up!

Knock Knock.
Who's there?
Fannie.
Fannie who?
Fannie body
home?

Knock Knock.
Who's there?
Felix.
Felix who?
Felix my ice cream,
I'll lick his!

Knock Knock.
Who's there?
Eileen.
Eileen who?
Eileen'd on your
bell and broke it.

Knock Knock.
Who's there?
Elsie.
Elsie who?
Elsie you later.

Knock Knock.
Who's there?
Enoch.
Enoch who?
Enoch and Enoch
but no one
answers the door.

Knock Knock.
  Who's there?
Ghost.
  Ghost who?
Ghost to show
you don't
remember my name!

Knock Knock.
  Who's there?
Ghandi.
  Ghandi who?
Ghandi cane.

Knock Knock.
  Who's there?
Genoa.
  Genoa who?
Genoa any new
jokes?

Knock Knock.
  Who's there?
Gorilla.
  Gorilla who?
Gorilla me a cheese
sandwich.

Knock Knock.
  Who's there?
Gladys.
  Gladys who?
Gladys is my last joke.

Knock Knock.
Who's there?
Hair.
Hair who?
Hair today, gone tomorrow.

Knock Knock.
Who's there?
Hannah.
Hannah who?
Hannah partridge in a pear tree.

Knock Knock.
Who's there?
Hawaii.
Hawaii who?
I'm fine. Hawaii you?

H

Knock Knock.
Who's there?
Harriet.
Harriet who?
Harriet up. We're going to be late!

Knock Knock.
Who's there?
Isabel.
Isabel who?
Isabel not working?

Knock Knock.
Who's there?
Idaho.
Idaho who?
Idaho'd the whole garden, but I got tired.

I

Knock Knock.
Who's there?
Ice cream soda.
Ice cream soda who?
Ice cream soda whole world will know how much I love you!

Knock Knock.
Who's there?
Ken.
Ken who?
Ken I come in?
It's cold out here!

Knock Knock.
Who's there?
Kenya.
Kenya who?
Kenya guess
who it is?

Knock Knock.
Who's there?
Kansas.
Kansas who?
Kansas the best
way to buy tuna.

Knock Knock.
Who's there?
Ketchup.
Ketchup who?
Ketchup with me
and you'll find out!

Knock Knock.
Who's there?
Kendall.
Kendall who?
Kendall and Barbie
go together.

Knock Knock.
  Who's there?
Lionel.
  Lionel who?
Lionel bite you if
you put your head
in its mouth!

Knock Knock.
  Who's there?
Lena.
  Lena who?
Lena little closer
and I'll tell you.

Knock Knock.
  Who's there?
Leaf.
  Leaf who?
Leaf me alone!

Knock Knock.
  Who's there?
Luke.
  Luke who?
Luke through the keyhole
and you'll see.

Knock Knock.
  Who's there?
Li'l ol'lady.
  Li'l ol'lady who?
I didn't know you
could yodel.

Knock Knock.
  Who's there?
Manuel.
  Manuel who?
Manuel be sorry if
you don't let him in.

Knock Knock.
  Who's there?
Marilyn.
  Marilyn who?
Marilyn is a state just
north of Virginia.

Knock Knock.
  Who's there?
Marietta.
  Marietta who?
Marietta whole cake!

Knock Knock.
  Who's there?
Mae.
  Mae who?
Mae be I'll tell you
and Mae be I won't.

Knock Knock.
  Who's there?
Mikey.
  Mikey who?
Mikey won't fit
in this lock.

Knock Knock.
Who's there?
Nadia.
Nadia who?
Nadia head if you understand what I'm saying.

Knock Knock.
Who's there?
Needle.
Needle who?
Needle little more time.

Knock Knock.
Who's there?
Noah.
Noah who?
Noah don't know who you are either!

Knock Knock.
Who's there?
Norma Lee.
Norma Lee who?
Norma Lee I don't go around knocking on people's doors, but I just had to meet you.

Knock Knock.
Who's there?
Nuisance.
Nuisance who?
Any nuisance I saw you yesterday?

Knock Knock.
  Who's there?
Olive.
  Olive who?
Olive you!

Knock Knock.
  Who's there?
Orange.
  Orange who?
Orange you going
to open this door?

Knock Knock.
  Who's there?
Ozzie.
  Ozzie who?
Ozzie you later.

Knock Knock.
  Who's there?
Pecan.
  Pecan who?
Pecan me again and
I'll tell the teacher!

Knock Knock.
  Who's there?
Phyllis.
  Phyllis who?
Phyllis in on the
news, please.

Knock Knock.
  Who's there?
Phillip.
  Phillip who?
Phillip my glass,
will you please?

15

Knock Knock.
Who's there?
Quack.
Quack who?
Quack another bad joke and I'm leaving.

Knock Knock.
Who's there?
Quilt.
Quilt who?
Quilt-ee as charged.

Knock Knock.
Who's there?
Qualify.
Qualify who?
I'll qualify ever want to tell you.

Q

Knock Knock.
Who's there?
Quarter.
Quarter who?
Quarter with her hand in the cookie jar!

Knock Knock.
Who's there?
Quebec.
Quebec who?
Quebec to the end of the line!

Knock Knock.
　Who's there?
Raleigh.
　Raleigh who?
Raleigh 'round
the flag, boys!

Knock Knock.
　Who's there?
Safari.
　Safari who?
Safari, so good.

Knock Knock.
　Who's there?
Rufus.
　Rufus who?
Rufus leaking and
I'm getting wet!

Knock Knock.
　Who's there?
Rhoda.
　Rhoda who?
Rhoda horse yesterday
and fell off.

Knock Knock.
　Who's there?
Sarah.
　Sarah who?
Sarah doctor
in the house?

Knock Knock.
　Who's there?
Rosa.
　Rosa who?
Rosa corn grow
in the field.

Knock Knock.
　Who's there?
Shirley.
　Shirley who?
Shirley you must
know me by now?

17

Knock Knock.
  Who's there?
Thea.
  Thea who?
Thea later,
alligator!

Knock Knock.
  Who's there?
Tank.
  Tank who?
You're welcome!

Knock Knock.
  Who's there?
Tinker Bell.
  Tinker Bell who?
Tinker Bell is
out of order.

Knock Knock.
  Who's there?
Tuna.
  Tuna who?
Tuna piano and it
will sound better.

Knock Knock.
  Who's there?
Tennis.
  Tennis who?
Tennis five
plus five.

Knock Knock.
  Who's there?
Uganda.
  Uganda who?
Uganda get
away with this!

Knock Knock.
  Who's there?
Utta.
  Utta who?
Utta sight,
Utta mind.

Knock Knock.
Who's there?
Usher.
Usher who?
Usher wish you would let me in.

Knock Knock.
Who's there?
Udder.
Udder who?
Udder people let me in, why won't you?

Knock Knock.
Who's there?
Uriah.
Uriah who?
Keep Uriah on the ball!

19

Knock Knock.
Who's there?
Viola.
Viola who?
Viola sudden don't you know me?

Knock Knock.
Who's there?
Vaughn.
Vaughn who?
Vaughn day my prince will come.

Knock Knock.
Who's there?
Voodoo.
Voodoo who?
Voodoo you think you are?

Knock Knock.
Who's there?
Verdi.
Verdi who?
Verdi been all day?

Knock Knock.
Who's there?
Van.
Van who?
Van can I see you again?

Knock Knock.
Who's there?
Who.
Who who?
Did you hear an owl?

Knock Knock.
Who's there?
Wah.
Wah who?
Gee, I didn't know you'd get so excited about it!

20

Knock Knock.
Who's there?
Xavier.
Xavier who?
Xavier breath,
I'm not leaving!

Knock Knock.
Who's there?
Xavier.
Xavier who?
Xavier money
for a rainy day.

Knock Knock.
Who's there?
X.
X who?
X for
breakfast.

Knock Knock.
Who's there?
Xenia.
Xenia who?
Xenia playing ball
at the park.

Knock Knock.
Who's there?
Warrior.
Warrior who?
Warrior been
all my life?

Knock Knock.
Who's there?
Wayne.
Wayne who?
Wayne who?
Wayne, Wayne
go away!

Knock Knock.
Who's there?
Waddle.
Waddle who?
Waddle you give
me if I go away?

21

Knock Knock.
  Who's there?
Yolanda.
  Yolanda who?
Yolanda me some
money?

Knock Knock.
  Who's there?
Ya.
  Ya who?
I didn't know
you were a cowboy!

Knock Knock.
  Who's there?
Yacht.
  Yacht who?
Yacht a know me
by now!

Knock Knock.
  Who's there?
Yellow.
  Yellow who?
Yellow my name is Katie.

Knock Knock.
  Who's there?
You.
  You who?
Did you call me?

22

Knock Knock.
  Who's there?
Zizi.
  Zizi who?
Zizi when you
know how.

Knock Knock.
  Who's there?
Zany.
  Zany who?
Zany body home?

Knock Knock.
  Who's there?
Zippy.
  Zippy who?
Mrs. Zippy.

Knock Knock.
  Who's there?
Zeke.
  Zeke who?
Zeke and you
shall find!

Knock Knock.
  Who's there?
Zone.
  Zone who?
Zone dog bit
him in the leg!

About Patrick Girouard:

Patrick Girouard has been illustrating books for almost 15 years but still looks remarkably lifelike. He loves reading, movies, coffee, robots, a beautiful red-haired lady named Rita, and especially his sons, Marc and Max. Here's an interesting fact: A dog named Sam lives under his drawing board. You can visit him (Patrick, not Sam) at www.pgirouard.com.

About Pam Rosenberg:

Pam Rosenberg is a former junior high school teacher and corporate trainer. She currently works as an author, editor, and the mother of Sarah and Jake. She took on this project as a service to all her fellow parents of young children. At least now their kids will have lots of jokes to choose from when looking for the one they will tell their parents over and over and over again!